COTSWOLDS TRAVEL GUIDE 2025

> "Plan the Perfect Cotswolds Getaway with Local Secrets and Must-See Attractions."

Charles Wesley

All rights reserved. No part of this publication may be reproduced, distributed, or transmitted in any form or by any means, including photocopying, recording, or other electronic or mechanical methods, without the prior written permission of the publisher, except in the case of brief quotations embodied in critical reviews and certain other noncommercial uses permitted by copyright law.

Copyright © Charles Wesley, 2025

Scan this QR CODE for an interactive map packed with detailed insights, hidden gems, and must-visit destinations across Cotswolds.

DISCLAIMER

The information provided in this guidebook is based on the author's personal experiences, research, and opinions. While every effort has been made to ensure the accuracy of the details included, some information may have changed since the time of writing.

The author and publisher are not responsible for any omissions, errors, or changes that may occur after the publication of this guide. Readers are encouraged to exercise caution and conduct further research when making travel plans.

If you have any questions, need clarification, or have suggestions for improving future editions of this guide, please don't hesitate to reach out. I am always happy to assist fellow travelers!

You can contact me directly at *CharlesWesleyTravels3@gmail.com* for inquiries or feedback.

Safe travels and happy exploring!

Charles Wesley

TABLE OF CONTENTS

Chapter 1: INTRODUCTION 11

1.1. Welcome to the Cotswolds: England's Countryside Gem 13

1.2. Why Visit in 2025? Exciting Updates and New Attractions 15

1.3. Understanding the Cotswolds: Geography, History, and Culture 16

1.4. Getting There: Best Routes from London and Other UK Cities 18

Chapter 2: PRACTICAL TRAVEL INFORMATION 20

2.1. Essential Packing List: What to Bring for Every Season 21

2.2. Currency, Costs, and Budgeting for Your Trip 24

2.3. Health and Safety: Emergency Numbers, Clinics, and Travel Insurance Tips 26

2.4. Local Etiquette: Dos and Don'ts for Travelers 28

Chapter 3: SUGGESTED ITINERARIES 31

3.1. The Perfect Weekend Escape: A Two-Day Classic Route 32

3.2. A Five-Day Cotswold Experience: Culture, Countryside, and Cuisine 35

3.3. A One-Week Adventure: Exploring the Cotswolds in Depth 38

3.4. Family-Friendly Itinerary: Kid-Friendly Activities and Destinations 39

3.5. Romantic Getaway: Cozy Retreats, Scenic Walks, and Candlelit Dinners 40

3.6. Off the Beaten Path: Secret Villages and Hidden Gems _____40

Chapter 4: TOP DESTINATIONS & HIGHLIGHTS _____ 42

4.1. Bibury: The Quintessential English Village ____43

4.2. Bourton-on-the-Water: The Venice of the Cotswolds _____45

4.3. Stow-on-the-Wold: History, Antiques, and Cozy Tea Rooms_____46

4.4. Chipping Campden: Arts, Architecture, and Thatched Cottages_____48

4.5. Castle Combe: A Timeless Fairytale Setting ____50

4.6. Broadway: The Jewel of the Cotswolds and Stunning Broadway Tower Views _____52

4.7. Stroud: Vibrant Markets, Local Arts, and Hidden Waterways _____54

4.8. Cirencester: The Capital of the Cotswolds and Roman Heritage _____56

4.9. Painswick: Rolling Hills, Historic Churches, and Tranquil Walks _____58

4.10. Hidden Gems: Underrated Villages and Secret Beauty Spots _____60

Chapter 5: TRANSPORTATION _____ 63

5.1. Getting to the Cotswolds: Trains, Buses, and Driving Tips _____64

5.2. Renting a Car vs. Public Transport: What's Best for You?_____66

5.3. Scenic Drives: Most Beautiful Routes in the Cotswolds _____68

5.4. Cycling the Cotswolds: Best Routes and Bike Rentals _____ 70

5.5. Walking and Hiking Trails: Navigating on Foot 71

Chapter 6: MUST-DO ACTIVITIES _____ 74

6.1. Exploring Historic Castles, Manor Houses, and Gardens_____ 75

6.2. Hiking the Cotswold Way: Iconic Trails and Best Walks _____ 77

6.3. Wildlife Encounters: Nature Reserves and Animal Parks_____ 79

6.4. Quaint Market Towns and Local Shopping Experiences _____ 80

6.5. Visiting Traditional Pubs and Experiencing Local Ale Culture_____ 81

6.6. Seasonal Events and Festivals _____ 82

Chapter 7: COTSWOLD CUISINE _____ 85

7.1. Traditional Dishes to Try: Local Flavors and Specialties _____ 86

7.2. Best Pubs and Restaurants: Where to Eat in the Cotswolds _____ 89

7.3. Farm Shops, Bakeries, and Food Markets _____ 91

7.4. Afternoon Tea and Cozy Cafés: A Quintessential Experience _____ 92

7.5. Vegan, Vegetarian, and Dietary-Friendly Options _____ 93

Chapter 8: CULTURAL INSIGHTS _____ 95

8.1. The Arts and Crafts Movement: Its Cotswold Legacy_____ 96

8.2. Historic Churches and Cathedrals: A Journey Through Time _____ 98

8.3. Folk Legends and Stories of the Cotswolds __ 100

8.4. Sustainability and Eco-Friendly Travel in the Cotswolds _____ 101

8.5. Photography Tips: Capturing the Best of the Cotswolds _____ 103

Chapter 9: ACCOMMODATION OPTIONS __ 106

9.1. Quaint Bed & Breakfasts and Family-Run Inns 107

9.2. Luxury Country Hotels and Boutique Stays __ 109

9.3. Farm Stays: Experience Life in the Countryside _____ 110

9.4. Eco-Lodges and Sustainable Accommodation Choices _____ 111

Chaoter 10: SPECIAL INTEREST TRAVELERS 114

10.1. Solo Travelers: Tips for an Independent Cotswold Adventure _____ 115

10.2. Family Travel: Kid-Friendly Attractions and Activities _____ 116

10.3. Luxury Travelers: High-End Experiences and Exclusive Stays _____ 118

10.4. Nature Lovers and Adventure Seekers: Best Outdoor Experiences _____ 119

Chapter 11: LOCAL LANGUAGE & COMMUNICATION _____ 121

11.1. Understanding the Cotswold Accent and Local Dialect _____ 122

11.2. Helpful English Phrases for International Travelers _____ 124

11.3. Wi-Fi, SIM Cards, and Staying Connected __ 125

Chapter 12: ESSENTIAL TRAVEL TIPS _____ 128

12.1. Best Apps for Exploring the Cotswolds _____ 129

12.2. Tipping Culture and Payment Methods _____ 131

12.3. Road Safety and Driving Rules for Visitors _ 133

12.4. Avoiding Tourist Traps and Common Scams 135

Chapter 13: CONCLUSION _____ 138

13.1. Final Travel Reminders: Ensuring a Smooth Trip _____ 139

13.2. Respecting Local Culture and Rural Traditions _____ 141

13.3. Eco-Friendly Travel Tips: Reducing Your Carbon Footprint _____ 142

13.4. The Future of the Cotswolds: Preserving Its Beauty for Generations to Come _____ 144

Chapter 1:
INTRODUCTION

The Cotswolds is one of England's most captivating destinations, offering you a glimpse into the country's rural charm with its rolling green landscapes, historic villages, and timeless stone cottages. Whether you are visiting for a weekend escape or planning a more extended trip, this area is a perfect mix of history, culture, and breathtaking scenery. Unlike the fast-paced atmosphere of London or the bustling energy of major UK cities, the Cotswolds invites you to slow down, explore at your own pace, and soak in the beauty of the English countryside. Every village has its unique character, every walking trail leads to something unexpected, and every local pub serves hearty food alongside centuries of tradition.

As you plan your 2025 journey, you will find that the Cotswolds offers more than just picturesque views. New attractions, seasonal festivals, and restored historic sites make this the perfect year to explore. Whether you're drawn to the charming high streets lined with boutique shops or looking for outdoor adventures across rolling hills and scenic footpaths, the Cotswolds is an experience waiting to be discovered. This introduction will guide you through the essential details to help you make the most of your trip, from understanding the region's geography and history to finding the best routes to get there.

1.1. Welcome to the Cotswolds: England's Countryside Gem

When you think of the English countryside, the Cotswolds are the image that comes to mind—stone-built villages, winding country roads, and a landscape that stretches for miles in every direction. This officially designated Area of Outstanding Natural Beauty (AONB) covers nearly 800 square miles and spans several counties, including Gloucestershire, Oxfordshire, Warwickshire, Wiltshire, and Worcestershire. Unlike other parts of England, the Cotswolds has retained much of its historical charm, making it one of the most sought-after destinations for travellers looking to experience traditional rural life.

You will wander through cobbled streets, past golden-hued buildings made from the region's signature limestone. It's a place where time seems to slow down, allowing you to appreciate the finer details of village life—tea rooms serving homemade scones, independent bookshops filled with rare finds and country lanes leading to breathtaking hilltop views. Whether it's your first visit or you're returning to explore more hidden corners, the

Cotswolds offers a tranquil and unforgettable experience.

1.2. Why Visit in 2025? Exciting Updates and New Attractions

Travelling to the Cotswolds in 2025 offers a fresh perspective on a region that constantly evolves while keeping its historical essence intact. This year brings several new attractions, updated visitor experiences, and seasonal highlights, making it an ideal time to explore. From newly restored historical sites to immersive cultural events, there's something for every traveller looking to experience the Cotswolds beyond its postcard-perfect villages.

The 2025 travel season will see the opening of new walking routes, including expanded sections of the Cotswold Way that provide better access to some of the most stunning landscapes in the region. Additionally, several historic manor houses and estates have undergone renovations, allowing visitors to explore previously inaccessible areas. Culinary enthusiasts will also have plenty to look forward to, with farm-to-table dining experiences and revived food festivals celebrating the best of Cotswold produce. Whether you're a history buff, an outdoor adventurer, or a food lover, 2025 offers new reasons to make the Cotswolds your next travel destination.

1.3. Understanding the Cotswolds: Geography, History, and Culture

The Cotswolds' landscape is shaped by rolling hills, scenic valleys, and ancient woodlands, making it one of the most breathtaking regions in England. As you explore, you'll notice the unique limestone architecture that gives the villages their warm honey-coloured glow—a signature feature of this part of the country. The region is divided into different sections, each with its distinct character, from the historic market towns of Gloucestershire to the quieter, less-explored corners of Warwickshire.

The history of the Cotswolds dates back centuries, with its wealth initially built on the medieval wool trade. Towns such as Chipping Campden and Stow-on-the-Wold were once thriving centres of commerce, and remnants of this past can still be seen in their grand market halls and elegant merchant houses. Beyond its economic history, the Cotswolds has long been a haven for artists, writers, and craftspeople. The Arts and Crafts Movement, which emphasized traditional craftsmanship, left a lasting impact on the region, particularly in villages like Broadway and Chipping

Campden. Today, the Cotswolds continues to celebrate its artistic heritage through galleries, workshops, and local craft fairs.

1.4. Getting There: Best Routes from London and Other UK Cities

Reaching the Cotswolds from London and other major UK cities is easier than ever, giving you multiple options depending on your travel style. If you prefer a scenic drive, renting a car offers excellent flexibility, allowing you to explore the countryside at your own pace. The journey from London takes approximately two hours via the M40 or M4, with beautiful routes leading you into the heart of the Cotswolds. Parking is available in most towns and villages, though it's always best to check in advance if you're visiting during peak tourist seasons.

For those relying on public transport, train services connect London Paddington to key Cotswold towns, including Moreton-in-Marsh, Kingham, and Cheltenham. Once you arrive, local buses and taxis can take you to smaller villages that aren't directly accessible by train. Similar rail and bus connections make the Cotswolds a convenient getaway if you're travelling from Birmingham, Oxford, or Bristol. No matter how you choose to arrive, the journey itself is an experience, offering glimpses of the charming countryside that awaits.

With all this in mind, your 2025 visit to the Cotswolds promises to be filled with incredible sights, rich history, and unforgettable moments. This guide will help you uncover the best of what the region offers, ensuring that your trip is nothing short of extraordinary.

Chapter 2: PRACTICAL TRAVEL INFORMATION

Travelling to the Cotswolds is an exciting experience, but proper preparation is key to ensuring a smooth and enjoyable trip. Unlike big cities, where everything is at your fingertips, the rural charm of the Cotswolds means that planning will save you time, money, and unnecessary stress. From unpredictable weather to different payment methods, understanding what to expect before you arrive will help you make the most of your journey.

This section will provide essential travel tips to enhance your 2025 adventure. Whether you need to know what to pack, how to budget for daily expenses, or what local customs to know, this guide ensures you are well-informed before stepping into England's most enchanting countryside.

2.1. Essential Packing List: What to Bring for Every Season

Packing for the Cotswolds depends on the season you plan to visit. The English countryside is known for its unpredictable weather, so being prepared for sudden changes will make your trip much more comfortable. A well-packed bag will prepare you for long country walks, charming village explorations, and relaxing afternoons in historic pubs.

If you visit in spring (March to May), expect mild temperatures with occasional rain showers. Waterproof walking shoes or boots are a must, especially if you plan on exploring the countryside trails. A lightweight waterproof jacket and an umbrella will come in handy, along with layers such as sweaters or fleece tops for cooler mornings and evenings.

Summer (June to August) in the Cotswolds brings warmer weather, but temperatures vary. Light, breathable clothing is ideal, but a light jacket or cardigan is recommended for breezy evenings. Sunglasses, sunscreen, and a reusable water bottle will keep you comfortable during longer outdoor excursions. If you plan to visit during peak tourist season, comfortable walking shoes are essential, as you'll likely spend hours strolling through villages and market towns.

Autumn (September to November) is a beautiful time to visit, with crisp air and golden foliage across the landscape. By late October, you'll need warm and waterproof clothing, including a mid-weight jacket, scarves, and gloves. This season is perfect for countryside hikes, so sturdy footwear is recommended.

Winter (December to February) in the Cotswolds can be magical, chilly, and occasionally snowy. A heavy coat, warm layers, a hat, gloves, and a scarf are necessary, especially if you plan to walk through open landscapes. Some villages, especially those at higher elevations, can experience frost and occasional ice, so non-slip footwear is a good idea.

No matter the season, a travel adapter for UK plugs (Type G), a portable phone charger, and a small backpack for day trips will make your travels easier. Consider bringing a smart-casual outfit to dining in upscale restaurants or attending theatre events.

2.2. Currency, Costs, and Budgeting for Your Trip

The currency used in the Cotswolds is the British Pound (£, GBP). While card payments are widely accepted, carrying some cash is advisable, particularly when visiting smaller villages, farmers' markets, or local events where cash may be preferred. ATMs are available in most towns, but you may not find them in more remote areas, so withdrawing money in advance is recommended.

Daily costs in the Cotswolds can vary depending on your travel style. If you're on a budget, expect to spend around £60–£80 per day, covering accommodation in budget-friendly inns, meals at local cafés, and entrance fees to some attractions. Mid-range travellers can expect to spend between £100–£200 per day, including stays in charming B&Bs, dining at quality restaurants, and enjoying activities like guided tours. For a luxury experience, your budget may range from £250 upwards, covering boutique hotels, fine dining, and exclusive experiences such as private countryside tours or spa retreats.

To save money, consider purchasing attraction passes or booking accommodations that include breakfast. Many pubs and cafés offer set menus or lunch deals, which can be a great way to experience high-quality meals at a lower cost.

Tipping is not mandatory in the UK, but it is appreciated. A 10–12.5% service charge is often included in restaurant bills. If not, a tip of around 10% is customary. Tipping in pubs is not expected, but you can offer to buy the bartender a drink instead. For taxi drivers, rounding up to the nearest Pound is common.

2.3. Health and Safety: Emergency Numbers, Clinics, and Travel Insurance Tips

Your health and safety should always be a priority when travelling, and the Cotswolds is no exception. While the region is generally safe, having the correct information at hand will ensure peace of mind throughout your trip.

For medical emergencies, dial **999** for an ambulance, police, or fire services. For non-urgent medical issues, dialling **111** will connect you to NHS services for advice on treatment or the nearest available doctor. Most towns have local clinics and pharmacies, with larger hospitals in cities like Cheltenham, Gloucester, and Oxford.

Travelling with comprehensive health insurance that covers medical emergencies, doctor visits, and prescription medications is recommended. If you're visiting from another country, check whether your insurance includes UK coverage or if you need to purchase additional travel insurance.

If you require regular medication, bring enough to last your trip and a copy of your prescription. Pharmacies in the UK provide over-the-counter medicines for minor ailments, but specific prescriptions may require a doctor's visit.

When exploring the countryside, be mindful of uneven terrain and weather conditions. Carry a basic first aid kit for minor injuries, and if you plan on hiking, inform someone of your route in case of emergencies. While crime rates are low in the Cotswolds, constantly monitor your belongings, especially in busy tourist areas.

2.4. Local Etiquette: Dos and Don'ts for Travelers

Understanding local customs and etiquette will help you connect with residents and make your visit more enjoyable. While the Cotswolds is a welcoming and relaxed destination, following a few basic rules will ensure you leave a positive impression.

Dos:

- **Greet locals politely.** A simple "hello" or "good morning" is always appreciated when entering shops, cafés, or small businesses.
- **Respect the countryside.** When hiking, stick to marked trails, close gates behind you on farmland, and avoid disturbing livestock.
- **Queue patiently.** The British are known for their queuing culture, so whether you're waiting for a bus or

ordering at a café, always wait your turn.

- **Support local businesses.** Shopping at independent stores, dining at family-run restaurants, and visiting farmers' markets contribute to the local economy.
- **Follow pub etiquette.** In traditional pubs, ordering drinks at the bar rather than waiting for table service is customary. If you're with a group, offering to buy a round of drinks is common.

Don'ts:

- **Don't be loud or disruptive.** The Cotswolds is a peaceful region, and loud behaviour, especially in small villages, is frowned upon.
- **Don't expect 24/7 convenience.** Many shops and restaurants close earlier than in big cities, with some

businesses shutting down in the late afternoon or early evening.
- **Don't pick flowers or damage wildlife.** Many areas in the Cotswolds are protected landscapes, so always leave nature as you find it.
- **Don't ignore local customs.** If visiting a historic site or church, dress appropriately and follow any posted guidelines.

By following these simple guidelines, you'll have a smoother experience and show respect for the people and places that make the Cotswolds such a unique destination.

With these practical travel tips, you're better prepared for your journey to the Cotswolds. Whether it's knowing what to pack, how to budget, or understanding local customs, a little preparation goes a long way in ensuring a memorable and hassle-free trip.

Chapter 3: SUGGESTED ITINERARIES

With its rolling hills, historic villages, and charming market towns, the Cotswolds offers endless opportunities for exploration. Whether visiting for a quick weekend escape or planning a more immersive journey, having a well-planned itinerary ensures you make the most of your time. The Cotswolds is not the kind of place where you rush from one attraction to the next. Instead, it's a region best enjoyed leisurely, allowing you to soak in the beauty, history, and atmosphere of each village and landscape.

To help you experience the Cotswolds in the best possible way, this section provides carefully designed itineraries tailored to different types of travellers. Whether you're interested in history, countryside walks, gourmet dining, or simply unwinding in a beautiful setting, you'll find an itinerary that suits your travel style. Each one is crafted to offer a balance of sightseeing, relaxation, and unforgettable experiences.

3.1. The Perfect Weekend Escape: A Two-Day Classic Route

If you only have a weekend to explore the Cotswolds, you'll want to focus on a selection of villages and landmarks that offer the most picturesque and memorable experiences. A two-day itinerary allows you to visit some of the region's most iconic destinations without feeling rushed.

Day One: Quintessential Cotswolds

Start your journey in Chipping Campden, one of the prettiest market towns in the region. Stroll along the historic High Street, lined with honey-coloured stone buildings, and visit the 17th-century Market Hall. Stop by Hidcote Manor Garden, a stunning National Trust property known for its beautifully designed outdoor spaces.

Continue to Broadway, often called the "Jewel of the Cotswolds." Walk up to Broadway Tower, a historic folly with panoramic views over the countryside. Enjoy lunch at a traditional country inn before driving to Snowshill, a tiny village with picture-perfect cottages. Visit Snowshill Manor, which houses an eclectic collection of artefacts.

Wrap up your first day in Bourton-on-the-Water, famous for its charming low bridges and riverside setting. Have dinner at a cosy gastropub before checking into a local B&B for a restful night.

Day Two: Historic Landmarks and Scenic Walks

Begin your second day in Stow-on-the-Wold, a historic wool town with antique shops, independent cafés, and a famous medieval church door at St. Edward's Church. From there, head to Lower Slaughter, where you can walk along the River Eye and visit the old water mill.

After lunch, spend your afternoon in Bibury, often called "the most beautiful village in England." Walk along Arlington Row, one of the most photographed streets in the country, before taking a scenic countryside drive back to your starting point.

3.2. A Five-Day Cotswold Experience: Culture, Countryside, and Cuisine

A five-day itinerary allows for a deeper exploration of the Cotswolds, balancing history, nature, and culinary delights.

Day One: Northern Cotswolds Highlights

Follow the weekend itinerary, visiting Chipping Campden, Broadway, Snowshill, and Bourton-on-the-Water, with an additional stop at The Slaughters, two of the region's most picturesque villages.

Day Two: History and Heritage

Spend a full day exploring Cirencester, the "Capital of the Cotswolds." Visit the Corinium Museum to learn about the town's Roman history before exploring Cirencester Park and its tree-lined avenues. In the afternoon, visit Tetbury, known for its antique shops and proximity to Highgrove Gardens, the private estate of King Charles III.

Day Three: Scenic Walks and Hidden Gems

Take a morning walk along the Cotswold Way, a long-distance trail offering breathtaking countryside views. Explore the peaceful village of Painswick, then drive to Minchinhampton and Rodborough Commons, where wild-roaming cattle graze.

Day Four: Food and Drink Experiences

Dedicate a day to sampling the best of Cotswold cuisine. Visit Daylesford Organic Farm for fresh produce, cheese tastings, and cookery classes. Have lunch in Kingham, home to award-winning restaurants. Spend your afternoon visiting local breweries or distilleries, such as the Cotswolds Distillery, where you can sample gin and whisky.

Day Five: Castles and Gardens

End your trip with visits to Sudeley Castle, a historic estate connected to Henry VIII's last wife, and Blenheim Palace, a UNESCO-listed masterpiece and the birthplace of Winston Churchill.

3.3. A One-Week Adventure: Exploring the Cotswolds in Depth

A seven-day itinerary allows you to experience the Cotswolds' rich history, natural beauty, and local culture without missing out on its hidden gems. In addition to the five-day itinerary, add:

- **A day in Stratford-upon-Avon**, the birthplace of William Shakespeare. Visit his childhood home, see a performance at the **Royal Shakespeare Theatre**, and explore the charming riverside.
- **An excursion to the southern Cotswolds**, visiting **Castle Combe**, often called England's prettiest village, and **Lacock**, a historic town frequently used as a filming location for movies and TV shows.
- **A full day in Bath**, a UNESCO World Heritage city known for its

Georgian architecture, Roman Baths, and elegant shopping streets.

3.4. Family-Friendly Itinerary: Kid-Friendly Activities and Destinations

Traveling with children? The Cotswolds offers many family-friendly attractions, from wildlife parks to interactive museums.

- **Cotswold Wildlife Park**: See giraffes, rhinos, and lemurs in a parkland setting.
- **The Model Village in Bourton-on-the-Water**: A miniature replica of the village, perfect for kids.
- **Cotswold Farm Park**: Get up close with farm animals and enjoy tractor rides.
- **Puzzlewood**: A magical forest that inspired Star Wars and Harry Potter scenes.

3.5. Romantic Getaway: Cozy Retreats, Scenic Walks, and Candlelit Dinners

Stay in a luxury countryside hotel or a cosy thatched-roof cottage for a romantic escape. Enjoy:

- Sunset views from Broadway Tower
- Afternoon tea at The Manor House in Castle Combe
- Horse-drawn carriage rides through the countryside
- Private hot tub stays in boutique lodges

End your evenings with candlelit dinners in atmospheric restaurants such as The Wild Rabbit in Kingham or The Painswick.

3.6. Off the Beaten Path: Secret Villages and Hidden Gems

For travellers seeking lesser-known spots, explore:

- **Naunton**, a secluded village with a medieval dovecote
- **Guiting Power**, a quiet town with fantastic countryside walks
- **The Rollright Stones**, an ancient stone circle with mysterious origins
- **The Slad Valley** inspiration for poet Laurie Lee's famous work

These hidden gems offer a peaceful escape from busier tourist areas, letting you experience the Cotswolds at its most authentic.

With these carefully curated itineraries, you can choose the best way to explore the Cotswolds, whether you're visiting for a short or a week-long adventure.

Chapter 4: TOP DESTINATIONS & HIGHLIGHTS

The Cotswolds is one of the most charming regions in England, filled with picturesque villages, historic market towns, and breathtaking countryside. Each destination has its unique character, from riverside walks and medieval churches to honey-coloured cottages and lively market squares. Whether you are seeking a peaceful retreat, cultural experiences, or scenic landscapes, the Cotswolds has a place that will captivate you.

This section highlights five must-visit destinations in the Cotswolds. These locations have long been favourites among travellers, offering stunning views, fascinating history, and plenty of things to see and do. If you plan your trip, these places should be on your list.

4.1. Bibury: The Quintessential English Village

Few places in England are as instantly recognizable as Bibury. With its iconic row of weavers' cottages, Arlington Row, this village looks like something out of a storybook. Bibury's charm is in its stone cottages, tranquil river, and lush green meadows, making it one of the most photographed spots in the country.

Begin your visit by exploring Arlington Row, a row of 17th-century cottages initially built as a wool store before being converted into housing for weavers supplying the local cloth industry. This picturesque lane is one of England's most iconic sights, and in 2025, efforts to preserve its heritage continue to ensure it remains a timeless attraction.

Take a walk along the **River Coln**, which flows gently through the village, providing a serene setting for a stroll. Stop by **Bibury Trout Farm**, one of England's oldest working trout farms, where you can feed the fish or catch your meal. If you visit in spring or summer, the meadows surrounding Bibury burst into vibrant colours, attracting artists and photographers worldwide.

For a relaxing afternoon, enjoy a meal at **The Swan Hotel**, a charming riverside inn serving traditional Cotswold cuisine. Whether you opt for a cream tea or a hearty Sunday roast, dining in this historic setting is a memorable experience.

4.2. Bourton-on-the-Water: The Venice of the Cotswolds

Known for its low-arched bridges crossing the River Windrush, Bourton-on-the-Water is one of Cotswolds' most beautiful and visited villages. The shallow, crystal-clear river running through the heart of the town gives it a peaceful yet lively atmosphere, perfect for strolling, dining, and sightseeing.

Begin exploring by walking along the riverbank, where charming stone cottages line the water's edge. The reflections of these historic buildings in the water create a postcard-perfect scene. The village is home to several attractions ideal for visitors of all ages. The Model Village, a one-ninth-scale replica of Bourton-on-the-Water, offers a fascinating look at how the village appeared in the 1930s.

Animal lovers will enjoy Birdland Park & Gardens, home to over 500 species of birds, including flamingos, owls, and penguins. For car enthusiasts, The Cotswold Motoring Museum is a must-visit, featuring a fantastic collection of vintage cars and memorabilia.

You will find plenty of dining options along the riverside. Whether you choose a cosy café for afternoon tea or a traditional pub for classic fish and chips, the setting enhances the experience.

4.3. Stow-on-the-Wold: History, Antiques, and Cozy Tea Rooms

Sitting at the highest point in the Cotswolds, Stow-on-the-Wold is a historic market town known for its charming streets, independent shops, and fascinating past. Once a major wool trading centre, this town has retained its historic character while offering a delightful mix of modern comforts and traditional charm.

Begin your visit in the town square, where you will find the old Market Cross, a reminder of Stow-on-the-Wold's medieval roots. The surrounding streets are filled with antique shops, galleries, and independent boutiques, making this an excellent place for treasure hunting. If you are a history enthusiast, step inside St. Edward's Church, famous for its fairytale-like wooden door flanked by ancient yew trees.

Stow-on-the-Wold is also known for its excellent dining options. Enjoy a traditional cream tea at The Old Bakery Tea Room, or visit The Porch House, England's oldest inn, for a meal in a historic setting. With its inviting pubs, cosy cafés, and historic streets, Stow-on-the-Wold is a perfect stop for those looking to experience the classic charm of the Cotswolds.

4.4. Chipping Campden: Arts, Architecture, and Thatched Cottages

Chipping Campden is one of the most architecturally stunning towns in the Cotswolds. With its well-preserved limestone buildings, medieval market hall, and strong connection to the arts and crafts movement, this town offers a unique mix of history, creativity, and scenic beauty.

Explore along the High Street, where golden-hued buildings house independent shops, tearooms, and historic landmarks. The Market Hall, built in 1627, is a testament to the town's rich trading history. If you are interested in the arts, visit the Court Barn Museum, which celebrates the influential Arts and Crafts movement that flourished here in the early 20th century.

One of the highlights of Chipping Campden is Hidcote Manor Garden, one of England's most famous gardens. It features beautifully designed outdoor "rooms" with vibrant plants and flowers. Another must-see is Kiftsgate Court Gardens, known for its breathtaking views over the surrounding countryside.

End your visit with a meal at The Eight Bells, a charming 14th-century pub offering classic British dishes in a cosy atmosphere. Whether you admire the town's historic architecture or explore its artistic heritage, Chipping Campden will leave a lasting impression.

4.5. Castle Combe: A Timeless Fairytale Setting

Often referred to as England's prettiest village, Castle Combe is a destination that transports you back in time. With its charming stone cottages, medieval bridges, and picturesque streets, this village feels untouched by modern life. It is no surprise, that Castle Combe has been used as a filming location for numerous movies and TV shows, including War Horse and Downton Abbey.

Walk through the village and admire the stone cottages adorned with climbing roses. Like many other villages, Castle Combe has no modern street signs, enhancing its old-world charm. The village's small but historic church, St. Andrew's Church, features a faceless clock, one of England's oldest working clocksining experiences; book a table at The Manor House, a five-star country hotel offering exquisite fine dining in a grand setting. Enjoy afternoon tea in a local tearoom if you want something more relaxed.

Castle Combe is also a great destination for walkers. The surrounding woodlands and countryside provide excellent trails leading to stunning viewpoints, making it a fantastic spot for photographers and nature lovers.

The Cotswolds are filled with enchanting villages and historic towns, but these five destinations stand out for their beauty, heritage, and unique experiences. Whether exploring picturesque riverside settings, wandering through medieval streets, or indulging in local flavours, each place offers something unique.

4.6. Broadway: The Jewel of the Cotswolds and Stunning Broadway Tower Views

Broadway is often called the "Jewel of the Cotswolds", and for good reason. This elegant village, with its wide high street, honey-coloured stone buildings, and charming independent shops, is one of the region's most refined and picturesque destinations. A perfect blend of history, culture, and countryside, Broadway offers something for every traveller, whether looking to explore historic sites, admire breathtaking views, or enjoy fine dining.

Broadway Tower is one of the village's standout attractions. It is a striking 18th-century folly perched on the second-highest point in the Cotswolds. In 2025, the tower remains one of the best places to take in sweeping views of the surrounding countryside, stretching as far as 16 counties on a clear day. The nearby Broadway Tower Country Park offers fantastic walking trails and opportunities to spot local wildlife, including the resident herd of red deer.

Broadway is also known for its vibrant arts scene. The Gordon Russell Design Museum celebrates the village's connection to craftsmanship and furniture design, while The Broadway Museum & Art Gallery showcases an impressive collection of historical artefacts and artwork. If you are visiting in summer, check out the annual Broadway Arts Festival, which features exhibitions, workshops, and performances throughout the village.

For a memorable meal, book a table at The Lygon Arms, a historic coaching inn that has hosted famous figures like Oliver Cromwell and King Charles I. Whether you are enjoying a countryside walk, browsing luxury boutiques, or simply soaking up the atmosphere of this charming village, Broadway is a must-visit destination.

4.7. Stroud: Vibrant Markets, Local Arts, and Hidden Waterways

Stroud offers a different side of the Cotswolds—one that is lively, creative, and deeply connected to its independent spirit. Known for its thriving arts scene, vibrant farmers' markets, and stunning landscapes, Stroud has become a hub for artists, foodies, and outdoor enthusiasts.

One of the main draws of Stroud is its award-winning **Stroud Farmers' Market**, held every Saturday. This market is a paradise for food lovers, offering everything from artisan cheeses and freshly baked bread to organic produce and homemade preserves. It is the perfect place to sample local delicacies and interact with friendly vendors who take pride in their products.

Stroud's artistic heritage is reflected in its numerous galleries and independent shops. The Museum in the Park, set within a beautiful 17th-century mansion, tells the story of Stroud's history through fascinating exhibits and artwork. For those interested in textiles, The Stroudwater Textile Trust looks at the town's wool industry heritage, which played a crucial role in the region's development.

For outdoor adventurers, Stroud's hidden waterways and rolling hills provide countless opportunities for exploration. The Stroudwater Navigation Canal, once an essential transport route, has been beautifully restored and offers peaceful walking and cycling paths. Nearby, the Five Valleys provide stunning landscapes for hikers, with winding trails leading through woodlands, meadows, and picturesque villages.

With its creative energy, thriving market culture, and access to breathtaking countryside, Stroud is an ideal stop for those looking to experience a different side of the Cotswolds.

4.8. Cirencester: The Capital of the Cotswolds and Roman Heritage

As the largest town in the Cotswolds, Cirencester is often called the "Capital of the Cotswolds". Its rich history, Roman heritage, and bustling town centre make it a fascinating place to explore. While many Cotswold villages are known for their small, quiet charm, Cirencester offers a lively and dynamic atmosphere with plenty of historical sites, excellent shopping, and cultural attractions.

Start visiting the Corinium Museum, one of the finest museums dedicated to Roman Britain. Cirencester was once the second-largest Roman town in England, known as Corinium, and this museum displays incredible mosaics, artefacts, and reconstructions that bring its ancient past to life. If you enjoy history, a walk through the remains of Cirencester Amphitheatre, one of the largest known Roman amphitheatres in Britain, is a must.

Beyond its Roman history, Cirencester boasts a thriving town centre filled with independent shops, boutiques, and cafés. The Market Place is the heart of the town, featuring a mix of historic architecture and modern eateries. The impressive Parish Church of St. John the Baptist, with its stunning Gothic tower, is a landmark worth visiting.

For those who love the outdoors, Cirencester Park, part of the Bathurst Estate, offers miles of walking trails in a beautifully maintained setting. Whether exploring Roman ruins, shopping for local crafts, or enjoying a scenic walk, Cirencester perfectly balances history and modern charm.

4.9. Painswick: Rolling Hills, Historic Churches, and Tranquil Walks

Painswick is one of the Cotswolds' most atmospheric and peaceful villages, known for its narrow streets, historic buildings, and beautiful countryside surroundings. Sitting atop a hill, this village offers breathtaking views of the surrounding valleys and is often considered one of the best places for scenic walks and quiet escapes.

One of the standout attractions in Painswick is St. Mary's Church, famous for its 99 ancient yew trees and striking churchyard. Legend has it that the Devil prevents the 100th tree from growing, adding an air of mystery to this historic site. The church is an architectural masterpiece with impressive stained-glass windows and a fascinating history dating back to the 14th century.

Painswick is also the gateway to The Painswick Rococo Garden, a hidden gem unlike any other garden in the Cotswolds. Designed in the 18th century, this whimsical garden features ornamental buildings, vibrant flower displays, and winding pathways leading to stunning viewpoints. In early spring, the garden becomes a spectacular sea of snowdrops, attracting visitors from all over the country.

For those who love walking, the Cotswold Way National Trail runs through Painswick, offering incredible routes with panoramic countryside views. A peaceful village with a rich history and stunning landscapes, Painswick is the perfect destination for those looking to slow down and experience the beauty of the Cotswolds at a relaxed pace.

4.10. Hidden Gems: Underrated Villages and Secret Beauty Spots

While the most famous Cotswold villages attract many visitors, plenty of hidden gems offer just as much charm without the crowds. If you are looking for off-the-beaten-path locations that still capture the essence of the Cotswolds, consider adding these lesser-known spots to your itinerary.

Snowshill is a tiny village with an enchanting atmosphere, known for its traditional cottages and beautiful countryside views. The main attraction here is Snowshill Manor, an eccentric country house filled with unusual collections of artefacts gathered by the former owner, Charles Wade. The surrounding gardens are equally impressive, offering peaceful walks with stunning floral displays.

Lower Slaughter and Upper Slaughter are two picturesque villages often overlooked by tourists. Their riverside settings, charming stone bridges, and old water mills provide a tranquil and romantic escape from the more crowded areas of the Cotswolds.

For those seeking dramatic scenery, Cleeve Hill is the highest point in the Cotswolds and offers breathtaking countryside views. It can stretch to the Malvern Hills and Wales on a clear day. This is a fantastic spot for hikers and photographers looking for panoramic landscapes.

The Cotswolds are filled with hidden beauty waiting to be discovered. Whether you venture into lesser-known villages or climb to scenic viewpoints, exploring these secret spots will give you a deeper appreciation of the region's charm and history.

Chapter 5:

TRANSPORTATION

The Cotswolds, with its rolling countryside, historic villages, and winding lanes, offers an idyllic escape from the hustle of city life. However, getting around this picturesque region requires careful planning, as public transport options can be limited in certain areas. Whether arriving from London, exploring by car, or opting for a more eco-friendly approach like cycling or hiking, knowing the best travel methods will ensure a smooth and enjoyable trip.

Unlike major cities with extensive public transportation networks, the Cotswolds relies on a combination of trains, buses, and country roads. Some of the most stunning villages are tucked away in remote locations, making car rentals or well-planned cycling routes essential for reaching specific destinations. However, for those who prefer a more relaxed journey, several scenic train routes and bus services connect key towns. If you visit in 2025, new transportation updates, road improvements, and potential electric vehicle charging stations may further enhance your travel experience.

5.1. Getting to the Cotswolds: Trains, Buses, and Driving Tips

Your journey to the Cotswolds will largely depend on your starting point. Travelling from London has multiple options, including train services, bus routes, and car rentals.

Trains are one of the most efficient ways to reach the Cotswolds. The most direct route from London is via the Great Western Railway (GWR), which operates from

London Paddington to Moreton-in-Marsh, one of the key gateway towns to the region. The journey takes around 1 hour and 30 minutes, making it a convenient choice for day trips or weekend getaways. Other significant towns with railway stations include Cheltenham, Stroud, and Kemble (for Cirencester). Purchasing a Railcard can reduce costs if you explore multiple locations.

Buses are a budget-friendly alternative, but they take longer and require connections. National Express and Megabus operate routes from London to Cheltenham and Gloucester, where you can take local buses to various villages. The Stagecoach West bus network serves the Cotswolds, but services can be infrequent in smaller towns, so always check the latest timetables before planning your journey.

If driving, be prepared for narrow country roads, steep hills, and limited parking in smaller villages. The M40 and M4 motorways provide good access from London, with key exits leading towards Oxford, Gloucester, and Cheltenham. Renting a compact car is advisable, as some village roads can be tight for larger vehicles. New for 2025, additional electric vehicle (EV) charging stations have been installed in popular areas, making eco-friendly travel more accessible.

5.2. Renting a Car vs. Public Transport: What's Best for You?

Whether to rent a car or rely on public transport depends on your itinerary, budget, and comfort level when driving on rural roads.

Renting a car gives you flexibility and access to remote villages, allowing you to explore hidden gems without being constrained by bus schedules. However, parking can be limited in some villages, and roads are often single-lane with blind corners. This may add stress if you are not used to driving in the UK, particularly on the left side. Major rental companies like Hertz, Enterprise, and Avis operate in Cheltenham and Oxford, offering petrol and electric vehicles.

Public transport, while more environmentally friendly, has limitations. Trains serve only certain towns and bus services can be sporadic. Public transport is a viable option if you visit only the larger cities like Cirencester, Cheltenham, and Stroud. However, a car or bicycle is better for exploring villages like Castle Combe, Lower Slaughter, or Snowshill.

If you prefer not to drive but still want flexibility, private tours, taxi services, and ride-sharing apps (such as Uber and Bolt) are options. However, taxis in the Cotswolds can be expensive, and availability is lower in rural areas. Booking in advance is always recommended.

5.3. Scenic Drives: Most Beautiful Routes in the Cotswolds

For those with a car, the Cotswolds offers some of the most breathtaking drives in England. Winding through golden-stone villages, green valleys, and historic landmarks, these routes are perfect for a leisurely road trip.

One of the most famous routes is the Romantic Road, a 50-mile journey from Cheltenham to Stratford-upon-Avon. This drive takes you through Winchcombe,

Broadway, Chipping Campden, and Stow-on-the-Wold, offering stunning countryside views and historic stops.

Another must-drive is the Burford to Bourton-on-the-Water route, passing through Bibury, often regarded as the most beautiful village in England. If you want a more remote and peaceful experience, the Stroud to Painswick route takes you through rolling hills, hidden valleys, and charming stone cottages.

For an elevated experience, head to Cleeve Hill, the highest point in the Cotswolds, where you can enjoy panoramic views stretching towards Wales. This drive is particularly stunning during sunrise and sunset.

5.4. Cycling the Cotswolds: Best Routes and Bike Rentals

Cycling is an excellent way to explore the Cotswolds, offering a slower, more immersive experience while reducing your environmental impact. The region is well-suited for cycling, with a mix of gently rolling hills and more challenging climbs for experienced riders.

One of the best cycling routes is the Cotswold Line Cycle Route. This route follows the train route between Oxford and Worcester, passing through Moreton-in-Marsh, Chipping Campden, and Broadway. It is ideal for those combining train travel with cycling.

Try the Bourton-on-the-Water to Lower Slaughter route for a shorter but rewarding ride. This picturesque 3-mile ride takes you along the River Windrush and past historic stone bridges.

Bike rentals are available in towns like Cheltenham, Moreton-in-Marsh, and Broadway. Companies such as Cotswold Bike Hire and Hartwells Cycle Hire offer road bikes, electric bikes, and hybrid options for different terrain preferences.

If you prefer guided cycling experiences, Cotswold Electric Bike Tours offers curated routes. These allow you to explore the countryside without the effort of pedalling up steep inclines.

5.5. Walking and Hiking Trails: Navigating on Foot

For those who love walking, the Cotswolds is one of the best destinations in England for scenic hikes, nature trails, and historical walks. The region is home to the Cotswold Way, a 102-mile walking route stretching from Chipping Campden to Bath, passing through rolling hills, ancient woodlands, and charming villages.

The Broadway Tower Circular Walk is a great option if you are looking for shorter walks. It offers stunning hilltop views and a manageable 3-mile loop. Another scenic route is the Winchcombe to Belas Knap trail, which leads to a Neolithic burial chamber with panoramic views of the Severn Valley.

For river walks, the Bourton-on-the-Water to Upper Slaughter path follows a gentle stream, providing a peaceful stroll between two of the Cotswolds' most picturesque villages.

Walking maps are available at most Cirencester, Cheltenham, and Moreton-in-Marsh visitor centres. If hiking in more remote areas, bring a fully charged phone, a GPS app, and suitable footwear, as some trails can be muddy and uneven, especially after rain.

With so many transport options in the Cotswolds, you can choose the best way to explore based on your travel style. Whether you prefer the freedom of driving, the sustainability of cycling, or the serenity of walking, each transportation mode offers its unique way to experience this stunning region.

Chapter 6: MUST-DO ACTIVITIES

The Cotswolds is not just about charming villages and scenic countryside—it's a region filled with activities that immerse you in its history, culture, and natural beauty. Whether you want to explore centuries-old castles, hike along iconic trails, experience authentic local markets, or sip traditional ales in a historic pub, the Cotswolds offers something for every traveller. This is a destination where you can step back in time at a medieval manor house in the morning, enjoy a leisurely countryside walk in the afternoon, and end your day at a lively festival or a cosy fireside pub.

For those seeking outdoor adventure, the Cotswold Way presents some of England's most breathtaking walking routes, while wildlife reserves allow you to get up close with rare and native species. Shopping enthusiasts will love the artisan goods in historic market towns, and beer lovers can enjoy the region's rich brewing heritage. If you're visiting in 2025, exciting festivals, seasonal events, and even newly restored historic sites ensure your trip will be packed with unforgettable moments.

6.1. Exploring Historic Castles, Manor Houses, and Gardens

No trip to the Cotswolds is complete without experiencing its grand castles and stately homes. These historic estates showcase incredible architecture and offer a glimpse into the lives of England's aristocracy and medieval rulers.

One of the most famous landmarks is Sudeley Castle, located near Winchcombe.

This stunning castle has ties to Henry VIII and is the final resting place of his sixth wife, Katherine Parr. The castle's beautifully maintained gardens, including the Queens' Garden, which blooms with over 80 varieties of roses, make it an essential stop for history and nature lovers alike.

For a classic example of a Cotswold manor house, Snowshill Manor is an unmissable attraction. This fascinating home, once owned by eccentric collector Charles Paget Wade, houses an extraordinary array of artefacts worldwide. Each room has intriguing antiques, from samurai armour to historical musical instruments.

Another must-see is Blenheim Palace, a UNESCO World Heritage Site outside Cotswolds in Woodstock. The birthplace of Sir Winston Churchill, this magnificent estate features Baroque architecture, extensive landscaped gardens, and an interactive exhibition dedicated to Churchill's life.

If you appreciate gardens, Hidcote Manor Garden, located near Chipping Campden, is one of England's finest. Designed by American horticulturist Major Lawrence Johnston, it is a delight to explore its intricate garden rooms, wildflower meadows, and carefully curated plant collections.

6.2. Hiking the Cotswold Way: Iconic Trails and Best Walks

For travellers who love the outdoors, hiking in the Cotswolds offers some of the best walking trails in England. The most famous is the Cotswold Way, a 102-mile long-distance path from Chipping Campden to Bath, passing through rolling hills, ancient woodlands, and breathtaking viewpoints.

If you're not up for the entire trail, several shorter sections provide excellent day hikes. The Broadway Tower Circular Walk is a fantastic option, offering panoramic views over the Cotswolds from one of its highest points. Another scenic walk is the Winchcombe to Belas Knap route, which takes you past a well-preserved Neolithic burial chamber with stunning views of the surrounding valleys.

For a riverside walk, the Lower Slaughter to Bourton-on-the-Water path follows a picturesque waterway, offering a peaceful and leisurely stroll between two of the region's prettiest villages. If you prefer guided walks, several local tour companies provide historical and nature-focused walking tours, giving more profound insight into the region's rich past.

6.3. Wildlife Encounters: Nature Reserves and Animal Parks

The Cotswolds is home to an array of wildlife parks and nature reserves, where you can spot everything from native British species to exotic animals.

A top destination for animal lovers is Cotswold Wildlife Park & Gardens, located near Burford. This expansive park is home to over 260 species, including rhinos, giraffes, and lemurs. The park's beautifully landscaped gardens provide a relaxing atmosphere for a day out, and the giraffe walkway offers a unique chance to get close to these majestic creatures.

For a more natural wildlife experience, Slimbridge Wetland Centre is a must-visit. This sanctuary is dedicated to conserving wetland birds and is home to thousands of migratory birds, including flamingos and Bewick's swans. If you visit in winter, you can witness the spectacular arrival of thousands of geese and swans from Arctic breeding grounds.

If you prefer spotting wildlife in the wild, Greystones Nature Reserve in Bourton-on-the-Water offers beautiful meadowland walks where you can see wild otters, kingfishers, and butterflies. The reserve is also home to an Iron Age roundhouse, adding a historical element to your visit.

6.4. Quaint Market Towns and Local Shopping Experiences

Shopping in the Cotswolds is an experience, with market towns offering everything from local crafts and antiques to artisan food and handmade goods.

Stroud Farmers' Market is one of the best places to experience a traditional market every Saturday. Recognized as one of the best in the UK, this market features stalls selling organic vegetables, homemade cheeses, and locally baked goods.

For antique lovers, Stow-on-the-Wold is a treasure trove of unique finds. Its antique shops, such as Tudor House Antiques and Baggott Church Street, are filled with vintage furniture, artwork, and collectables. If you're looking for high-end local craftsmanship, head to Cirencester, often called the capital of the Cotswolds. Here, you'll find Cox & Baloney, a boutique shop filled with handmade jewellery, textiles, and ceramics from local artists.

6.5. Visiting Traditional Pubs and Experiencing Local Ale Culture

No trip to the Cotswolds would be complete without visiting a traditional English pub. The region is renowned for its historic inns, cosy fireplaces, and locally brewed ales.

One of the most famous pubs is The Porch House in Stow-on-the-Wold. It is considered England's oldest inn, dating back to 947 AD. The pub's charming low beams, roaring fire, and excellent selection of local ales make it an essential stop for travellers.

The Swan Inn in Bibury is an excellent choice for a riverside setting. Overlooking the River Coln, this pub serves delicious Cotswold-brewed beers and hearty British dishes.

For those interested in brewing, visiting Donnington Brewery near Stow-on-the-Wold offers a glimpse into traditional brewing techniques that have remained unchanged for centuries.

6.6. Seasonal Events and Festivals

The Cotswolds hosts an exciting calendar of events throughout the year, from literary festivals to food fairs and historical re-enactments.

If you're visiting in the spring, don't miss the Cheltenham Festival (March 2025), one of the UK's most significant horse racing events.

Summer brings the Cotswold Show & Food Festival (July 2025) in Cirencester, featuring live cooking demonstrations, artisan food stalls, and traditional country fair attractions.

For literature lovers, the Cheltenham Literature Festival (October 2025) attracts famous authors, poets, and speakers worldwide.

Winter is the perfect time to experience Christmas markets, with Blenheim Palace's Christmas Lights Trail and Bath's famous Christmas Market offering a magical festive atmosphere.

Whether you're drawn to history, outdoor adventures, wildlife encounters, shopping, or food, the Cotswolds offers a wide variety of experiences that will make your trip truly unforgettable.

Chapter 7: COTSWOLD CUISINE

The Cotswolds is a paradise for food lovers, offering a mix of traditional English dishes, artisanal produce, and contemporary dining experiences. Whether savouring a rustic countryside meal in a centuries-old pub, indulging in an elegant afternoon tea, or exploring bustling farm shops filled with fresh local ingredients, the region's culinary scene is as diverse as its landscape. The Cotswolds takes pride in farm-to-table dining, with many eateries sourcing ingredients directly from local farmers and producers. From hearty meat pies and creamy cheeses to delicate pastries and fine-dining creations, there's something to suit every taste.

As you explore the Cotswolds, you'll find that food is deeply intertwined with the region's identity. The area is home to some of the best cheesemakers, bakers, and brewers in England, with an emphasis on sustainable and organic produce. Whether you're a meat lover, a vegetarian, or someone with specific dietary needs, the Cotswolds offers an array of options that celebrate traditional flavours and modern innovations. To help you experience the best of Cotswold cuisine, here's a guide to the dishes you must try, the best dining spots, and the local markets that bring this region's flavours to Life.

7.1. Traditional Dishes to Try: Local Flavors and Specialties

When visiting the Cotswolds, indulging in its signature dishes is a must. The region is known for its rich agricultural heritage, producing everything from award-winning cheeses and cured meats to fresh baked goods and hearty stews.

One of the most iconic foods in the area is Gloucester Old Spot Pork, a rare breed pig known for its superior flavour. Many local pubs serve Gloucester Old Spot sausages with mash, gravy, and caramelized onions, perfectly embodying classic British comfort food.

Another must-try is Cotswold Lamb, which benefits from the region's lush pastures. Often served roasted with seasonal vegetables and rosemary-infused jus, this dish is a staple at many fine dining establishments and traditional inns.

You'll want to sample Double Gloucester and Stinking Bishop if you enjoy cheese. Double Gloucester is a rich, nutty cheese often used in cheese and onion pies or served on a rustic ploughman's platter with crusty bread and pickles. Stinking Bishop, on the other hand, is a strong-smelling but creamy and delicious washed-rind cheese that pairs beautifully with local ciders.

For a casual treat, try a Cotswold cream tea featuring freshly baked scones with clotted cream and strawberry jam—best enjoyed in a charming tearoom with a pot of English tea.

Finally, don't leave without tasting a Bath Bun or a Lardy Cake. The Bath Bun, originating from nearby Bath, is a sweet, enriched dough bun topped with sugar and crushed sugar lumps. At the same time, Lardy Cake is a traditional sticky, fruit-filled pastry that is surprisingly light and incredibly indulgent.

7.2. Best Pubs and Restaurants: Where to Eat in the Cotswolds

The Cotswolds is home to some of England's most charming, historic pubs and contemporary restaurants that highlight modern British cuisine.

For an authentic country pub experience, The Wild Rabbit in Kingham is a must-visit. This Michelin-starred gastropub takes a farm-to-table approach, serving dishes such as Cotswold venison, wood-roasted cod, and foraged mushroom risotto. The rustic yet refined setting makes it an excellent leisurely lunch or dinner place.

Another excellent spot is The Ebrington Arms, which has been repeatedly voted one of the best pubs in the UK. Known for its homemade pies, Sunday roasts, and award-winning ales, this 17th-century inn provides the perfect mix of tradition and quality.

For fine dining, Le Champignon Sauvage in Cheltenham offers an unforgettable experience. This Michelin-starred restaurant serves contemporary British cuisine with French influences, featuring roast duck with black garlic and Cotswold honey.

If you're in Bourton-on-the-Water, try The Slaughters Manor House, a fine-dining restaurant offering seasonal tasting menus with expertly paired wines.

Daylesford Organic Farm Café near Kingham serves fresh, organic dishes made with ingredients sourced from the café's farm for a casual yet high-quality meal. These include wood-fired pizzas, salads, and homemade pastries.

7.3. Farm Shops, Bakeries, and Food Markets

Food lovers will appreciate the Cotswolds' bustling farm shops and artisan bakeries, where they can buy local cheeses, fresh bread, and handmade preserves.

One of the best places to explore is Daylesford Organic Farm Shop, a renowned farm-to-table destination that offers everything from fresh organic produce and locally sourced meats to homemade soups and pastries.

For a genuine farmers' market experience, Stroud Farmers' Market is a must-visit. Every Saturday, this award-winning market features local cheeses, organic vegetables, handmade chocolates, and artisan bread.

If you have a sweet tooth, Huffkins Bakery, with locations in Stow-on-the-Wold and Burford, is known for its delicious Lardy

Cake, freshly baked scones, and traditional Cotswold shortbread.

7.4. Afternoon Tea and Cozy Cafés: A Quintessential Experience

Afternoon tea is a beloved British tradition, and the Cotswolds offers some of the best places to enjoy.

For a luxurious experience, Ellenborough Park in Cheltenham offers an elegant afternoon tea with finger sandwiches, homemade scones, and a selection of fine teas. You can enjoy your tea in a historic setting with views of the surrounding Countryside.

If you prefer a cosy village tearoom, Lucy's Tearoom in Stow-on-the-Wold serves a classic cream tea with homemade jam, clotted cream, and an excellent selection of cakes.

Another delightful spot is The Bridge Tea Rooms in Bradford-on-Avon, housed in a 17th-century building with old-world charm. This award-winning tearoom is known for its Victoria sponge cake and loose-leaf teas in bone china cups.

7.5. Vegan, Vegetarian, and Dietary-Friendly Options

The Cotswolds has embraced the growing demand for plant-based and dietary-friendly dining, offering various excellent vegan and vegetarian options.

The Coconut Tree in Cheltenham offers Sri Lankan-inspired vegan curries, jackfruit kottu, and coconut-based desserts for an entirely plant-based menu.

If you're looking for a vegetarian-friendly gastropub, The Green Dragon in Cowley serves beetroot tartare, wild mushroom stroganoff, and lentil shepherd's pie.

For gluten-free and allergy-friendly dining, The Hive in Stow-on-the-Wold offers an extensive menu with gluten-free cakes, dairy-free options, and organic vegetarian dishes.

Whether you indulge in a traditional Cotswold dish, enjoy a cream tea in a historic tearoom, or discover vegan-friendly dining spots, the region's food scene promises a memorable culinary experience.

Chapter 8: CULTURAL INSIGHTS

The Cotswolds is more than rolling hills and picture-perfect villages—a region steeped in culture, history, and artistic heritage. From the legacy of the Arts and Crafts Movement to ancient churches that whisper stories of medieval times, a deep cultural richness is waiting to be explored. Whether you are interested in local folklore, historical landmarks, or sustainability efforts shaping the future of travel, the Cotswolds offers a unique and immersive experience.

Understanding the region's cultural essence allows you to appreciate its traditions, architecture, and artistic contributions. As you wander through market towns filled with artisan shops, step inside centuries-old cathedrals, or listen to local legends passed down for generations, you will gain a profound sense of the Cotswolds' identity. This chapter highlights the key cultural experiences that will deepen your appreciation of this enchanting destination.

8.1. The Arts and Crafts Movement: Its Cotswold Legacy

The Cotswolds played a significant role in the Arts and Crafts Movement, a design philosophy that emerged in the late 19th century as a reaction against industrialization. Spearheaded by figures such as William Morris and Ernest Gimson, this Movement sought to revive traditional craftsmanship, emphasizing handmade over machine-produced goods.

You can experience this artistic heritage firsthand in Chipping Campden, which became the hub of the Movement thanks to the Guild of Handicrafts. The Court Barn Museum provides an insightful look at the works of skilled artisans, from handcrafted furniture to exquisite metalwork. Another must-visit is Kelmscott Manor, William Morris's former home, where you can admire original textiles, wallpapers, and furnishings that reflect his artistic vision.

Today, the Arts and Crafts legacy thrives in local workshops and galleries. Many villages host independent artists creating pottery, textiles, and jewellery inspired by the Movement's principles. Exploring these workshops not only supports local artisans but also provides an opportunity to take home a unique piece of Cotswold craftsmanship.

8.2. Historic Churches and Cathedrals: A Journey Through Time

The Cotswolds is home to some of England's most impressive churches and cathedrals, offering a glimpse into the region's religious and architectural history. From towering Gothic cathedrals to quaint village churches, these sacred spaces reflect centuries of devotion and artistry.

Gloucester Cathedral is one of the most renowned sites. It is an awe-inspiring medieval architectural masterpiece. Its intricate fan vaulting, stained-glass windows, and cloisters have captivated visitors for centuries. If you are a fan of cinematic history, you may recognize it from scenes in the Harry Potter films.

Another must-see is St. Mary's Church in Fairford, known for its extraordinary collection of medieval stained-glass windows that have miraculously survived through the ages. Cirencester's St. John the Baptist Church, often called the "Cathedral of the Cotswolds," boasts a stunning 15th-century tower and intricate tombs that reveal the wealth and status of wool merchants from bygone eras.

While exploring smaller villages, you will find charming parish churches, each with a story to tell. Painswick's St. Mary's Church is famous for its 99 ancient yew trees, while St. Edward's Church in Stow-on-the-Wold features a mystical, Tolkien-esque north door framed by twisted trees. These historical sites offer a sense of tranquillity and timeless beauty that enhance your journey through the Cotswolds.

8.3. Folk Legends and Stories of the Cotswolds

Beyond its scenic beauty, the Cotswolds is rich with folklore and legends that add a layer of intrigue to its historic landscape. Every village has its tales, passed down through generations, which reflect the beliefs and superstitions of the past.

One of the most famous stories is that of the "Wicked Lady," a 17th-century highwaywoman who is said to haunt the ruins of Swainswick near Bath. According to legend, she was a noblewoman by day and a ruthless thief by night until her eventual betrayal and demise.

Another eerie tale surrounds the Rollright Stones, a mysterious Neolithic stone circle. Local legend claims that the stones are a petrified king and his knights, cursed by a witch, to remain frozen in time. Visitors often report an inexplicable feeling of energy when standing among the ancient stones.

The Cotswolds is also home to the legend of the Stow Fair Ghost, said to be the spirit of a tragic young woman who roams the streets during the annual horse fair. Whether you believe in these tales or enjoy the storytelling tradition, these local legends add a fascinating dimension to the region's history.

8.4. Sustainability and Eco-Friendly Travel in the Cotswolds

With increasing awareness of sustainable travel, the Cotswolds has made significant strides toward eco-friendly tourism. Many local businesses and accommodations embrace environmentally conscious practices to preserve the region's beauty for future generations.

You can contribute to sustainable tourism by choosing eco-friendly lodgings, such as The Green Dragon in Cockleford, which focuses on energy efficiency and locally sourced food. Many countryside retreats now offer solar-powered accommodations, refillable toiletries, and farm-to-table dining experiences.

Public transport options, including buses and bike rentals, provide a greener alternative to driving, while designated walking trails encourage exploration without environmental impact. Shops and markets emphasize locally produced goods, reducing carbon footprints and supporting regional farmers.

Visitors are encouraged to respect the Countryside by following the Countryside Code—sticking to marked trails, minimizing waste, and respecting local wildlife. Whether opting for an electric vehicle rental or participating in a community-led conservation project, your choices can positively impact the Cotswolds' sustainability efforts.

8.5. Photography Tips: Capturing the Best of the Cotswolds

With its golden-stone villages, rolling hills, and picturesque landscapes, the Cotswolds is a dream destination for photographers. Knowing the best locations and times to shoot will elevate your photos, whether you're an amateur or a professional.

Early mornings offer the best light, with a soft glow enhancing the honey-coloured cottages and quiet streets free from crowds. Bourton-on-the-Water, known as the "Venice of the Cotswolds," is particularly stunning at dawn, when the reflections in the water create a mirror-like effect.

For landscape shots, head to Broadway Tower for panoramic views across multiple counties. The golden hour before sunset bathes the fields in warm, ethereal light, making it ideal for capturing the quintessential Cotswold scenery.

If you prefer close-up photography, the intricate details of ancient doors, stone carvings, and market stalls provide fascinating subjects. The autumn months bring a vibrant palette of reds and oranges to the woodlands, while winter transforms the villages into magical snow-dusted scenes.

By understanding composition techniques, playing with different angles, and embracing natural light, you can create stunning images that reflect the charm and character of the Cotswolds.

From historic arts and folklore to eco-conscious travel and photography, the

Cotswolds offers a cultural experience beyond its visual appeal. Immerse yourself in these stories and traditions as you explore to fully appreciate the depth of this extraordinary region.

Chapter 9: ACCOMMODATION OPTIONS

The Cotswolds is a region where traditional charm meets modern luxury, offering an array of accommodation choices that cater to every type of traveller. Whether you're seeking a cosy, family-run bed & breakfast, an opulent countryside hotel, or an eco-conscious retreat surrounded by rolling hills, you'll find the perfect place to stay. Accommodation in the Cotswolds is not just about finding a place to sleep; it's about immersing yourself in an experience that reflects the region's heritage, tranquillity, and hospitality.

As you plan your 2025 visit, consider what kind of stay best aligns with your travel style. Do you prefer the warmth of a personally hosted inn where homemade breakfasts and friendly conversations are part of the experience? Or is a boutique hotel with elegant interiors and top-tier amenities more your speed? Maybe you're drawn to waking up to the sounds of farm animals and enjoying fresh produce straight from the fields. No matter your preference, the Cotswolds has an accommodation option that will make your trip unforgettable.

9.1. Quaint Bed & Breakfasts and Family-Run Inns

For an authentic English countryside experience, nothing compares to a charming bed & breakfast or a historic family-run inn. These accommodations offer a personal touch, where warm hospitality and home-cooked breakfasts set the tone for your stay. Many B&Bs are housed in centuries-old cottages, often adorned with exposed wooden beams and roaring fireplaces, providing a cosy retreat after exploring.

In 2025, some of the best-rated B&Bs include The Old Stocks Inn in Stow-on-the-Wold, where modern elegance meets 17th-century character, and The Slaughters Country Inn, a delightful riverside property in Lower Slaughter. If you prefer a smaller, family-operated inn with an intimate atmosphere, The Lamb Inn in Burford offers a peaceful setting and classic English cuisine. Booking in advance is recommended, especially during peak seasons, as these charming properties are in high demand.

9.2. Luxury Country Hotels and Boutique Stays

For those seeking indulgence and sophistication, the Cotswolds boasts an impressive collection of luxury country hotels and boutique accommodations. These hotels often blend historic charm with contemporary amenities, ensuring a comfortable and memorable stay. Think four-poster beds, exquisite fine dining, and spa treatments that take relaxation to the next level.

The iconic Ellenborough Park, set in a stately 15th-century manor, remains one of the region's premier luxury stays, featuring a world-class spa and direct access to Cheltenham Racecourse. Another outstanding choice is Barnsley House, renowned for its impeccable gardens, boutique spa, and gourmet dining experiences. Meanwhile, Thyme, a country retreat in Southrop, offers an immersive experience combining fine accommodation, a cookery school, and farm-to-table dining. Whether you're celebrating a special occasion or want to treat yourself, these establishments promise an exceptional stay.

9.3. Farm Stays: Experience Life in the Countryside

If you want to connect with the rural side of the Cotswolds, a farm stay can provide an unforgettable experience. These accommodations allow you to embrace countryside living, where you can wake up to fresh farm air, help feed animals, or even try your hand at traditional farming activities. Farm stays are particularly popular among families and travellers who appreciate a rustic yet comfortable atmosphere.

Notable options include Abbey Home Farm in Cirencester, a working organic farm that offers stylish eco-lodges and cosy yurts, and Cotswold Farm Park, owned by TV presenter Adam Henson, which provides an educational yet relaxing farm experience. Daylesford Farm's cottages offer a high-end take on rural stays, combining organic food, wellness experiences, and chic interiors for those who want luxury while still being close to nature. Whether looking for a hands-on farm adventure or a peaceful retreat surrounded by nature, farm stays are a unique way to experience the Cotswolds.

9.4. Eco-Lodges and Sustainable Accommodation Choices

Sustainable travel is gaining traction, and the Cotswolds has embraced eco-conscious tourism by offering accommodations that prioritize sustainability without compromising comfort. Eco-lodges, green hotels, and environmentally friendly cottages have become increasingly popular, providing a guilt-free way to enjoy the region's natural beauty.

The Fish Hotel in the Farncombe Estate is a fantastic, eco-conscious stay that combines woodland cabins with a low-impact philosophy. Meanwhile, The Greenhouse at Daylesford provides a carbon-neutral retreat powered by renewable energy and surrounded by organic farmland. If you're interested in an off-grid experience, The Log House in Kingham offers an idyllic setting with solar power and a commitment to sustainability. Choosing one of these accommodations ensures that you support responsible tourism while enjoying a luxurious and relaxing stay.

From quaint B&Bs to luxury estates and eco-friendly retreats, the Cotswolds offers various accommodations tailored to different preferences and budgets. Whichever option you choose, you'll be surrounded by the region's stunning landscapes, warm hospitality, and a sense of timeless charm that will make your trip truly special.

Chaoter 10: SPECIAL INTEREST TRAVELERS

The Cotswolds is an incredibly diverse destination that appeals to many travellers. Whether you are venturing out alone, planning a trip with your family, seeking luxury experiences, or immersing yourself in outdoor adventures, this region has something unique to offer. Each type of traveller will find unique ways to enjoy the Cotswolds, with tailored experiences that ensure a truly memorable journey.

The region's rolling Countryside, historic villages, and charming accommodations provide the perfect backdrop for any travel style. Independent travellers can embrace a slower pace, exploring at their leisure. Families will appreciate interactive attractions, while luxury travellers can indulge in the finest cuisine and five-star country retreats. On the other hand, nature lovers and thrill-seekers can take advantage of the many walking trails, cycling routes, and wildlife encounters. No matter what brings you to the Cotswolds, an experience is waiting to capture your imagination and inspire your journey.

10.1. Solo Travelers: Tips for an Independent Cotswold Adventure

Travelling solo in the Cotswolds offers a sense of freedom and discovery that is difficult to replicate elsewhere. The region is safe, welcoming, and well-suited for independent exploration. You can set your own pace, stopping to admire the golden-stone villages, picturesque landscapes, and cosy cafes. Walking trails like the Cotswold Way allow for peaceful reflection, while market towns like Stow-on-the-Wold and

Cirencester provide friendly interactions with locals and fellow travellers.

For solo travellers, staying in a charming bed and breakfast or boutique hotel offers comfort and the opportunity to meet like-minded visitors. Public transport, while not as extensive as in urban areas, is still manageable for those without a car, with regular bus routes connecting significant villages. If you prefer a more immersive experience, consider joining a guided walking tour or booking a small-group workshop, such as pottery-making or countryside foraging, to interact with others while enjoying the region's traditions.

10.2. Family Travel: Kid-Friendly Attractions and Activities

Families travelling to the Cotswolds will find plenty of engaging activities to keep children entertained. The region boasts a mix of outdoor adventure, historical attractions, and interactive experiences designed for all ages. The Cotswold Wildlife Park and Gardens near Burford is a must-visit, allowing children to see animals like rhinos, penguins, and lemurs in a spacious, beautifully landscaped setting.

For hands-on activities, Cogges Manor Farm provides a delightful glimpse into traditional farm life, complete with friendly animals and play areas. The Cotswold Motoring Museum in Bourton-on-the-Water is another hit with families, featuring vintage cars and the beloved Brum character from the classic children's TV series. Outdoor-loving families can explore the Sculpture Trail in the Forest of Dean or enjoy a boat trip along the Thames in Lechlade.

10.3. Luxury Travelers: High-End Experiences and Exclusive Stays

If you seek luxury, the Cotswolds delivers an exceptional experience filled with fine dining, exclusive stays, and tailored activities. The region is home to some of England's most prestigious country hotels, including Cliveden House, Barnsley House, and Whatley Manor, where world-class spas and gourmet restaurants elevate your stay.

For an unforgettable dining experience, indulge in Michelin-starred cuisine at restaurants such as Le Champignon Sauvage in Cheltenham or The Wild Rabbit in Kingham. Private tours, from vineyard visits to hot air balloon rides over the Countryside, provide a unique regional perspective. Many estates offer VIP access, allowing guests to enjoy behind-the-scenes experiences like truffle hunting or wine tastings led by expert sommeliers.

10.4. Nature Lovers and Adventure Seekers: Best Outdoor Experiences

The Cotswolds is a paradise for outdoor enthusiasts, offering everything from gentle countryside strolls to adrenaline-fueled activities. The Cotswold Way, a 102-mile national trail, provides stunning panoramic views and passes through charming villages, making it perfect for long-distance hikers. Shorter scenic routes, such as the Broadway Tower walk or the circular trails around Painswick Beacon, cater to those looking for a leisurely yet rewarding trek.

Cycling is another excellent way to explore the Countryside, with dedicated routes like the Winchcombe Cycling Loop or the Thames Path National Trail. For those seeking adventure, the Cotswolds Water Park offers kayaking, paddleboarding, and wakeboarding, while hot air balloon rides provide breathtaking views of the rolling hills and historic landmarks. Wildlife lovers can visit the Slimbridge Wetland Centre, home to various bird species and conservation efforts, or join a guided nature tour to spot deer, foxes, and rare butterflies in the region's many nature reserves.

No matter your travel style, the Cotswolds offers a tailored experience that caters to your interests, ensuring an enriching and unforgettable journey.

Chapter 11: LOCAL LANGUAGE & COMMUNICATION

While the Cotswolds are a quintessentially English region, they have their own unique linguistic quirks and communication nuances that can add to the charm of your visit. Whether you are an international traveller looking to grasp useful English phrases or interested in the distinctive Cotswold accent and local expressions, understanding how people speak in this part of England will enrich your experience. The locals are known for their friendliness, and a basic understanding of their dialect and mannerisms will go a long way in fostering warm interactions.

In the digital age, staying connected while travelling is a priority for many. Whether you need Wi-Fi for navigation, social media updates, or work commitments, the Cotswolds offers various ways to ensure you remain online. From local SIM cards to accessible hotspots in cafes and hotels, this section will guide you through the best ways to communicate effectively during your trip.

11.1. Understanding the Cotswold Accent and Local Dialect

The Cotswold accent is a variation of the West Country dialect, with distinct inflexions that differ from the standard British accent you might be familiar with. While it has softened over the years due to modernization and migration, you may still hear traces of traditional speech patterns, especially in rural villages.

One of the key features of the accent is the dropping of the letter 'r' at the end of words (similar to Received Pronunciation) but with a slightly more drawn-out, lilting tone. Additionally, some older phrases and words persist in everyday conversation. For example, locals might refer to a small lane as a "twitten" or use "gurt" instead of "great." "Where be you too?" means "Where are you?"—a remnant of old English influences.

While you don't need to master the dialect, embracing a few local expressions will undoubtedly bring a smile to a Cotswold resident's face. Engaging with how people speak is also an excellent way to appreciate the region's heritage and storytelling traditions, which are still strong in local pubs and community gatherings.

11.2. Helpful English Phrases for International Travelers

If English is not your first language, you'll find that most locals speak clearly and are willing to help if you have trouble understanding. However, some common British phrases and expressions may be helpful during your stay:

- "Cheers!" – Used instead of "thank you" or when raising a toast.
- "Fancy a cuppa?" – An invitation to have a cup of tea.
- "Mind the gap" – A phrase often heard in transport settings, meaning be cautious of the space between the train and the platform.
- "It's a bit nippy out" – A casual way to say it's cold.
- "Pop to the shops" means quickly going to the store.

- "Could you point me in the right direction?" – A polite way to ask for directions.

Understanding these phrases will help you feel more comfortable and engaged in everyday conversations. British politeness is also key—saying "please," "thank you," and "excuse me" will always be appreciated.

11.3. Wi-Fi, SIM Cards, and Staying Connected

Staying connected in the Cotswolds is relatively easy, although rural areas may have weaker signals than more prominent towns and cities. Here are some key points to consider:

- **Wi-Fi Access**: Most hotels, cafes, and restaurants offer free Wi-Fi, but you may need to ask for a password. Though speeds can vary, some train stations and public spaces also have complimentary internet access.

- **Local SIM Cards**: Purchasing a UK SIM card is a cost-effective option if you need continuous mobile data. Providers like EE, Vodafone, O2, and Three offer prepaid SIMs with data packages suitable for short-term travellers. Ensure your phone is unlocked before purchasing a local SIM.
- **eSIM Options**: Travelers with eSIM-compatible devices can activate a UK data plan before arrival. Services like Airalo and Holafly offer flexible packages without needing a physical SIM card.
- **Roaming Charges**: If you travel from another country, check with your mobile provider about roaming fees. Some international plans

include free data usage in the UK, but others may charge high rates.

If you plan to explore off-the-beaten-path locations, downloading offline maps from Google Maps or apps like Maps.me will help you navigate areas with weak signal coverage. Additionally, messaging apps like WhatsApp and Telegram are widely used in the UK, making them convenient options for staying in touch with locals and fellow travellers.

With these tips, you can confidently communicate and stay connected during your journey through the Cotswolds, ensuring a smooth and enjoyable experience.

Chapter 12: ESSENTIAL TRAVEL TIPS

Traveling to the Cotswolds in 2025 promises to be an unforgettable experience, whether you explore charming villages, hike scenic trails, or indulge in traditional English cuisine. However, to make the most of your trip, you must be well-prepared with the right tools, understand local customs, and know essential safety tips. From using the most helpful travel apps to learning how to handle payments and avoid tourist pitfalls, these tips will ensure a smooth and stress-free journey.

Understanding the practicalities of travelling in the Cotswolds will allow you to enjoy its countryside charm without hassle. Unlike major cities, rural areas may have limited transport options, fewer cash machines, and varying road conditions. With these insights, you can confidently explore the region like a seasoned traveller, avoiding common mistakes and making informed decisions. Whether renting a car, searching for Wi-Fi, or simply wondering about tipping etiquette, this guide covers you.

12.1. Best Apps for Exploring the Cotswolds

In 2025, having the right travel apps on your phone will make exploring the Cotswolds much easier. While Wi-Fi is available in hotels, cafés, and some public places, a reliable mobile data plan will help you stay connected in more remote areas.

- **Google Maps and Citymapper** – Google Maps remains the best navigation tool for the Cotswolds, offering real-time traffic updates, walking routes, and public transport information. For those using buses or trains, Citymapper can be a helpful alternative for planning routes between towns.

- **National Trust App**—The National Trust manages many historic sites and walking trails in the Cotswolds. Its app provides details on opening hours, special events, and membership benefits.
- **Ordnance Survey App** – Ideal for hikers, this app provides highly detailed maps of the Cotswolds, ensuring you never lose your way on countryside walks.
- **The AA App** – If you are driving, this app provides road condition updates, fuel station locations, and emergency breakdown assistance.

- **Google Translate** – While English is the primary language, some local phrases may be unfamiliar. This app can assist international travellers with quick translations.
- **OpenTable and Resy** – Many restaurants in the Cotswolds require reservations, especially during peak travel seasons. These apps allow you to book tables in advance and explore reviews.
- **Trainline and Stagecoach Bus App**—For those relying on public transport, these apps provide up-to-date train and bus schedules and ticket purchasing options.

12.2. Tipping Culture and Payment Methods

Tipping in the UK is generally more relaxed compared to countries like the United

States, but it is still appreciated in many situations. While tipping is not mandatory, understanding when and how much to tip will help you blend in with local customs.

- **Restaurants and Cafés** – If a service charge is not included, leaving a tip of around 10-12% is standard practice. Tipping is not expected in casual cafés and pubs where you order at the counter.
- **Hotels**—A small tip of £1-£2 per service is a nice gesture, though not obligatory, for porters or housekeeping staff.
- **Taxis and Ride–Shares:** It is common to round up the fare to the nearest pound or add a small tip if the driver provides exceptional service.
- **Tour Guides** – Tipping around £5-£10 per person is appreciated if you

take a guided tour, especially for private or small-group tours.

Regarding payment methods, card payments are widely accepted across the Cotswolds. Contactless payment is the preferred method in most places, including public transport. However, some small businesses, market stalls, and village pubs may still operate on a cash-only basis, so carrying a small amount of cash is recommended.

12.3. Road Safety and Driving Rules for Visitors

If you rent a car to explore the Cotswolds, understanding UK driving laws and local road conditions is essential for a safe trip.

- **Driving on the Left**—In the UK, traffic flows on the left-hand side of the road. If you are used to driving on the right, this can take some adjustment.

- **Narrow Lanes and Country Roads** – Many rural roads in the Cotswolds are narrow, with hedgerows and blind corners. Drive cautiously and be prepared to slow down or pull over to let oncoming vehicles pass.
- **Speed Limits** – The general speed limit is 30 mph (48 km/h) in villages and towns, 60 mph (97 km/h) on rural roads, and 70 mph (113 km/h) on motorways and dual carriageways. Speed cameras are standard, so be mindful of posted limits.
- **Parking Regulations**—Parking restrictions apply in busy tourist areas. Look for designated parking areas and always check for signs indicating time limits or fees.

- **Roundabouts** – The UK uses roundabouts extensively. Give way to traffic approaching from the right unless directed otherwise.
- **Drinking and Driving** – The UK has strict laws against drunk driving, with a legal blood alcohol limit of 80 mg per 100 ml of blood. It is best to avoid drinking if you are driving.

For those unfamiliar with driving in the UK, consider renting an automatic vehicle to reduce the complexity of shifting gears while adjusting to left-side driving.

12.4. Avoiding Tourist Traps and Common Scams

While the Cotswolds is a relatively safe and welcoming destination, it is wise to be aware of potential tourist traps and minor scams that could impact your experience.

- **Overpriced Souvenirs** – Many shops in tourist-heavy areas charge inflated prices for souvenirs. Look for authentic handmade goods at local markets and independent stores instead.
- **Fake Discounts and Tours** – Some attractions and tour providers may advertise "exclusive" discounts that are not significantly cheaper than standard rates. Always check official websites for accurate pricing.
- **ATM Fees**—Some standalone cash machines charge high withdrawal fees. To avoid excessive charges, use bank ATMs where possible.
- **Restaurant Service Charges** – Some restaurants add a discretionary service charge. Check before tipping to avoid double-paying.

- **Pushy Street Vendors** – While not common in the Cotswolds, some tourist areas may have street vendors selling overpriced or low-quality items. Politely decline if you are not interested.
- **Accommodation Scams**: To avoid fraudulent listings, book accommodation using reputable platforms like Booking.com, Expedia, or official hotel websites.

Being prepared with these essential travel tips will allow you to focus on enjoying the stunning landscapes, charming villages, and rich cultural heritage of the Cotswolds. With the proper knowledge, you can travel confidently, make informed choices, and create lasting memories in this remarkable part of England.

Chapter 13:
CONCLUSION

The Cotswolds is not just a destination; it is an experience that will stay with you long after you leave. The rolling countryside, charming villages, and historic landmarks blend relaxation, adventure, and cultural enrichment perfectly. Whether wandering through the streets of ancient market towns, savouring a traditional English cream tea, or hiking the scenic trails that define this Area of Outstanding Natural Beauty, the Cotswolds promises a journey filled with unforgettable moments. Every season paints a different picture, from the golden hues of autumn to the vibrant blossoms of spring, ensuring that no two visits are identical.

As you prepare for your journey, remember that the Cotswolds is more than just a collection of postcard-worthy landscapes—it is a living, breathing region with a rich history and a close-knit community that takes pride in preserving its traditions. By travelling thoughtfully, respecting the environment, and embracing the local culture, you contribute to the ongoing story of this enchanting region. The Cotswolds will always have something new to discover and enjoy, whether it is your first visit or a return trip.

13.1. Final Travel Reminders: Ensuring a Smooth Trip

Before setting off, double-check your itinerary, accommodation bookings, and transportation plans. While the Cotswolds offers excellent public transport options, having a flexible schedule maximizes your time. If you are driving, familiarize yourself with villages' narrow country lanes and parking facilities. Packing appropriately for the season is essential; waterproof clothing and sturdy walking shoes are recommended year-round, as the weather can be unpredictable.

Ensure you have all necessary travel documents, including travel insurance if applicable. If you plan on using a rental car, carry your valid driver's license and review UK road regulations. Mobile connectivity is generally good, but some rural areas may have limited signal, so downloading maps and offline guides beforehand is a good idea. Above all, allow yourself time to truly experience the Cotswolds rather than rushing from one attraction to another.

13.2. Respecting Local Culture and Rural Traditions

The Cotswolds are deeply rooted in tradition, with many villages maintaining customs that date back centuries. As a visitor, being mindful of local etiquette enhances your experience and fosters positive interactions with residents. Simple gestures, such as greeting shopkeepers and acknowledging fellow walkers on countryside paths, go a long way. If you visit historic churches or landmarks, respect their significance by keeping noise levels low and following any posted guidelines.

Local farmers and landowners are vital in maintaining the region's stunning landscapes. When exploring the countryside, stick to designated footpaths, close gates behind you, and avoid disturbing livestock. Many villages have limited commercial development to preserve their charm, so support small businesses by dining at local restaurants, shopping at independent boutiques, and purchasing handmade crafts.

13.3. Eco-Friendly Travel Tips: Reducing Your Carbon Footprint

Sustainable travel is crucial in preserving the natural beauty of the Cotswolds for future generations. You can minimize your environmental impact while exploring the region in several ways. Opt for eco-friendly accommodations prioritizing sustainability, such as farm stays, converted barns, or lodges using renewable energy. Use public transport, rent bicycles, or walk between attractions instead of relying on a car when possible. Many villages are close enough to explore on foot, offering a more immersive experience while reducing carbon emissions.

Reducing waste is another key consideration. Carry a reusable water bottle and coffee cup, as many local cafes offer discounts for bringing your container. Avoid single-use plastics by shopping at local markets that use minimal packaging. When dining out, choose restaurants that source ingredients from local farms and sustainable suppliers. Participating in conservation efforts, such as supporting organizations that maintain footpaths or volunteering for local environmental projects, is another meaningful way to give back.

13.4. The Future of the Cotswolds: Preserving Its Beauty for Generations to Come

The Cotswolds is a place of timeless beauty, but its future depends on responsible tourism and conservation efforts. Climate change, increased visitor numbers, and modern development challenge the region's delicate ecosystem. Practising mindful travel, you help protect the landscapes, wildlife, and heritage that make the Cotswolds so unique.

Local organizations, such as the Cotswolds Conservation Board and the National Trust, are essential in preserving the area's historical sites and natural reserves. Supporting these initiatives through donations, memberships, or participation in educational programs helps ensure that the Cotswolds remains a destination of unparalleled charm. Travellers can also contribute by respecting local guidelines, avoiding overcrowded hotspots during peak times, and encouraging others to adopt responsible tourism practices.

Every journey to the Cotswolds should leave it as beautiful as it was found. By embracing sustainable travel, appreciating local culture, and engaging with the region's heritage, you become part of the ongoing effort to safeguard this remarkable destination. Whether visiting for a short getaway or an extended stay, your experience in the Cotswolds will be richer when approached with care, curiosity, and respect.

Get In Touch With Charles Wesley

Thank you for allowing this guidebook to accompany you on your adventures. I hope it has inspired, informed, and enriched your experience as you discover the incredible places within its pages.

If you have any questions, need further insights, or would like to share your travel experiences, I would love to hear from you! Your feedback helps improve future editions and ensures that other travelers can embark on even more fulfilling journeys.

Please feel free to contact me at **CharlesWesleyTravels3@gmail.com** with your inquiries, thoughts, or stories. Whether it's a small question about a hidden gem, practical tips, or just a kind word about how this guide helped you, I am always happy to connect with fellow adventurers.

Safe travels and unforgettable adventures,

Your guide and fellow traveler,

Charles Wesley
Email: **CharlesWesleyTravels3@gmail.com**

Printed in Dunstable, United Kingdom